Legal Reference Library
Volume I

by
John Philip Mason

While we have done our best to give you useful and accurate information in this book, the publisher and the author do not accept responsibility for any interpretation or application by the reader of this book. Laws change frequently and are subject to different interpretations. If you want legal advice backed by a guarantee, you should hire an attorney. This book is not a substitute for an attorney, and it does not attempt to answer all questions about every situation you may encounter. The publisher and author urge the reader to consult an attorney for appropriate advice on specific legal situations as circumstances dictate.

SANTA MONICA PRESS
P.O. Box 1076
Santa Monica, CA 90406-1076
Printed in the United States
All Rights Reserved

Contents

Introduction

You probably have many questions about the legal system. You're probably fascinated and intrigued by it, and you hope to find out more about how justice is served in this country.

But on a more somber note, you probably feel like the law is beyond you. After all, it takes years just to learn how to pronounce all of those funny words, let alone understand what they mean. Perhaps you sometimes get confused when watching those courtroom dramas on the television. And maybe you've even been confronted with a contract which contains fine print that is both baffling and frightening.

Well, I've got good news for you. The legal system in America today is not about learning the definitions of 12-syllable words. It is not some secret and exclusive world, filled with a jargon all its own, where the general public is not invited. On the contrary, the legal system is made for ordinary folks, people like you and me. Now, don't get me wrong. I'm not trying to tell you that you'll be qualified to be the lawyer on a murder trial once you're through reading the *Legal Reference*

Library. But you will have a solid understanding of some of the most common applications of the law. Examples of these applications include your rights and responsibilities as a motorist, how to plan out a will, and the legal consequences of owning a home.

The first, and most important, thing you need to know about law is that it is not something you need to be frightened of. Sure, contracts can be intimidating sometimes, but they are essentially just a list of rules. The legal system in America today is simply a set of rules designed to enable people to argue in a structured and orderly fashion, so that justice can be served. This type of justice applies not only to the high profile trials we see on the news, but also to the kinds of problems faced by you and me. For example, if you hire someone to paint your house, and he does a lousy job, you have certain legal rights. These rights have been created in the name of justice (i.e., it is just that your house should be painted well if you paid someone to do it). But in order for justice to be served, you need to have some understanding of the rules of the law. *The Legal Reference Library* will help you attain that basic level of understanding.

Okay, so the law is essentially a set of rules, like the rules in a football game. And it's not that hard to figure out that the judge is kind of like the referee. But in a football game, the referee makes his decisions based on the quality of the team's play. How does a judge make his decision? What do you need to do in order for justice to be served?

The answer to that question is simple! All you have to do is prove to the judge that someone has broken the rules. Using the example of the painter once again, you would simply explain to the judge that you paid someone to paint your house, but they did not do an adequate job. *The way that you can use the law is by arguing effectively.* That's really all that lawyers are: expert arguers. They know how to analyze a conflict and prove that justice needs to be served.

If you've ever had the chance to look at legal documents before, then you might be familiar with words like "form interrogatories," "document production," and "memorandum of points and authorities." These words are the titles that lawyers give to their legal documents. While I won't go into detail here explaining exactly what these titles mean, I can assure you that they are all simply documents that a lawyer uses in order to analyze a conflict and argue a point effectively to a judge. That is all that you need to do in order to conquer the legal system! So now do you believe me when I say that there is nothing to be scared about?

At this point, I do want to point out that you should never allow yourself to get in over your head when using the law. After all, top lawyers are experts at their craft, and they would run circles around you in court! So, use your common sense: hire a lawyer when necessary. Let's hope none of us ever get wrongfully charged of committing murder, for example, but it would probably be a sensible idea to hire a good lawyer if that ever happened!

I also want to give you a warning about how to use the *Legal Reference Library*. Although every attempt has been made to write in plain, easy-to-understand English, you will most likely be learning new concepts. As a result, don't try to skim through these volumes in one or two nights. Read them slowly. Give yourself time to digest the ideas. If there is something you don't understand, read it over again once or twice. Don't move on to a new concept until you are ready. As I have tried to express throughout this introduction, the law is made for you and me. It is not beyond our abilities, but it does take some getting used to, so don't rush things. And don't worry if you find something a little tricky to understand every now and then!

So, without further ado, let's turn to chapter one and start learning how we can protect your rights!

1

Why, When, and How To Use the Legal System

This first chapter will deal with the nuts and bolts of the legal system. That is, you will learn how to find a lawyer, how to take someone to court, etc. You will find an awful lot of information crammed into a relatively small space, so don't be alarmed if you don't understand everything the first time around. Moreover, you won't need to know all of this information for every legal situation that you might ever find yourself in. For example, if you ever decide to set up a will, then you will not need to go to court in order to do so. In other words, this section of the book is designed to give you an overview of the entire legal system, but chances are you will never have to know *all* of this material.

In order to get started, let's answer some of the most common questions asked about the American legal system.

Question:
So why should I use the legal system? What can it do for me?

Answer:
You should use the legal system as a means of resolving conflict. A conflict is any incident

that occurs which causes two or more people to have a disagreement. If, for example, you get into a fender-bender while driving your car, and you have a disagreement with the other driver over who should pay for the damages, then you have a conflict.

The legal system can provide a solid set of rules for you to resolve the conflict. If you have ever gotten into a serious argument with someone, then you probably got very emotional about the situation. The person with whom you were arguing also probably got very emotional, which made it difficult for you to resolve the situation. The reason it was so difficult is because you did not have a solid set of rules by which to come to an agreement; you allowed your emotions to get in the way of reason. The legal system prevents this from happening by ensuring that conflicts are settled under strict guidelines which are supervised by an impartial judge. Think of a judge as somewhat like a teacher, settling the disputes of schoolchildren by listening carefully to what each student says the other did wrong.

You can also use the legal system as a means of preventing conflict. If, for example, you want to make sure that a certain member of your family receives the title to your house when you pass away, then you must clearly say so in a will. That way, after the time of your death, you can be sure that that family member has received your house, and that no one else has the right to stake a claim to it. If someone else did try to stake a claim to it, then a conflict would occur. Thus, the legal system also provides a solid set of rules in order to prevent conflicts.

So what the legal system can do for you is make sure that justice is served. You might have heard the old saying, "No one can escape the long arm of the law." That saying is very true. If you know how to use the legal system, then you will not have any problems getting a quick and fair trial.

Question:

But unless I have millions of dollars with which to hire a highly paid attorney, the legal system is probably beyond my means, isn't it?

Answer:

Actually, the legal system is not beyond the means of any of us! Unlike the legal systems of most other countries, the American legal system is designed to be as fair and impartial as possible. Therefore, it doesn't make any difference if you are rich or poor, young or old. All of us can obtain solid legal representation if we just know how to do so. This book will show you how. In fact, as you will discover shortly, there are even certain courts in the country, called Small Claims Courts, which insist that you argue your case on your own, without the assistance of a lawyer.

At this point, it is important to note that this book will focus on civil issues, rather than criminal ones. If you are not familiar with these terms, then you will learn more about them later in this chapter. You should be aware, however, that if you are ever arrested by the police for breaking the law, then they will "read you your rights." One of your rights is free legal representation if you cannot afford it. Therefore, if you do not have very much money, you will still have access to competent legal services.

Question:

Can I use the legal system to "strike it rich?"

Answer:

No! Never, ever use the legal system as a way of taking advantage of people! Unfortunately, all too many people these days seem to have the idea that they can sue someone in court for no reason whatsoever and make a bundle of money. This is called lawsuit abuse, and it is a very serious problem in America today.

Here is why you should not continue the trend of lawsuit abuse. First, if the judge decides that you are abusing the legal system, not only will you lose your case, but you will also be subject to some very heavy fines. People have been fined over $100,000 for abusing the legal system! Second, you tie up court time, which prevents other trials from being presented to a judge as quickly as possible. This means that people who are involved in a valid conflict have no way of resolving it in a speedy way, which is unfair to them. And finally, lawsuit abuse costs tax payers millions of dollars each year. You see, judges and other court officials are paid by state and federal taxes, and if they are being paid to preside over frivolous trials, then our tax money is going to waste.

This does not mean that there is never a valid reason to sue someone for lots of money. Sometimes people have a valid reason for suing others for large sums of money. If you were ever hit by a car, for example, your medical bills could be quite high, so you would probably sue the driver for the cost of your treatment.

Question:
Does the legal system ever make a mistake? What can I do if I have a legitimate conflict, but for some reason the judge rules against me?

Answer:
One of the biggest fears that most people have about using the legal system is that they might be getting in over their head. People with legitimate conflicts sometimes never resolve them because they are scared that they might "put their foot in their mouth" while in the courtroom, thereby preventing themselves from winning a trial they deserved to win.

Well, judges are aware that most people get nervous when they enter a courtroom (you might have heard the old saying that "only a guilty man looks innocent"). Admittedly, however, sometimes mistakes are made. But if this happens to you, then you need not worry. You see, the American legal system allows you to "appeal" any decision made by a judge. If you appeal a decision, then another judge takes a second look at the case, and sees if the first judge might have made an error.

If you have any fears about utilizing the legal system, just try to remember that judges try to be as fair and impartial as possible, and that they will honestly try to work with you to ensure that justice is served. They are not scary and imposing figures who have no time for you. In fact, they are paid by your tax dollars, so their time is your time!

How To Find an Attorney

Most people do not know how to go about finding a lawyer. Ironically, obtaining a lawyer is one of the easiest processes you can go through.

The simplest, and most common, way to search for a lawyer is through the Yellow Pages. If you open your Yellow Pages to the caption entitled "Attorneys," you will probably find hundreds of names listed there. You might as well just start at the top of the list and work your way down, until you have found someone who you think will best represent your interests.

The way you determine if a lawyer will best represent your interests is by telling him or her a little bit about your conflict and asking him or her questions. Here are a few questions that you should ask:

1. Have you ever handled a case like mine before?

2. What is your success rate?

3. Can I get some references from satisfied clients?

4. How much do you charge per hour, and can you give me an estimate of any other costs or fees for which I might be liable?

5. Will I receive a monthly bill, or will you take a contingency? (A "contingency" is a percentage of any money that you win in court. If, for example, you get hit by a car,

and you successfully prove in court that the driver was at fault, then you will probably win some money.)

6. If you will take the case on contingency, will I have to pay a retainer? If so, how much? (A "retainer" is an up-front sum of money that the lawyer will ask for in order to tide him over until he wins the case for you and receives the contingency.)

7. Can I speak with you in person about my case, in order to help determine whether you are the right lawyer for me? If so, will you charge me any money for this initial consultation?

If you do not have any luck finding a suitable lawyer through the phone book, then the next resource to turn to is the American Bar Association. By law, all lawyers practicing in America today have to belong to this association (you will learn why in a few moments). As a result, the Bar Association has a "Lawyer Referral Service" which will be able to refer you to lawyers specializing in cases similar to yours. They will probably give you a list of several lawyers to call, so you should be sure to ask each lawyer the same questions that were listed above. The phone number for the American Bar Association can be found through the phone book or through directory assistance.

The reason why all lawyers belong to the American Bar Association is because this is the organization that regulates them. Every now and then, a lawyer turns out to be dishonest, and he or she might even try to steal some money from a client. If you are unlucky enough to hire a lawyer who turns out to be a crook, then simply call up the Bar Association, and they will help you get your money back, as well as seeing to it that the dishonest lawyer never gets to practice law again!

Small Claims Court

In order for the legal system to function as smoothly as possible, disputes are placed into different types of categories. As mentioned earlier, the most basic type of category is civil versus criminal. Within the realm of civil trials, the simplest forum for resolving disputes is referred to as small claims court.

Two things separate small claims court from

any other courts of law. First, the maximum amount of money that can be disputed over is $5,000. This means that if you get into a fender bender, and the bill amounts to $5,000 or less, then you qualify for small claims court. And second, you are not allowed to have a lawyer present at the time of the trial. This does not mean that you cannot consult with a lawyer beforehand, in order to work out the best legal strategy, but the lawyer cannot actually accompany you to court. However, the fees that lawyers charge for such consultations are often so high that they outweigh the benefits of seeking legal advice.

If you consider yourself to be the "victim" of a conflict (in the example of the fender bender, the person whose car was hit by someone else), then you will sue someone else. Suing someone merely means that you are asking them to meet you in a court of law in order to resolve the dispute before an impartial judge. If you ever decide to sue someone else, then you are referred to as the "plaintiff." The person who you are suing is referred to as the "defendant."

But before you ever try to sue anyone, you should always try to resolve the situation outside of a court first. Always attempt these resolutions in writing, so that you will have evidence (or proof) that you have done so. In the example of the fender bender, assuming the other person does not have insurance, you should write to them and very politely ask that they pay for your car repair bill. A sample of such a letter follows:

Your name
Your address
Your phone number

The date

The other person's name
The other person's address

Dear Other Person:

You and I were involved in a fender bender on {date the incident occurred}. Regrettably, that incident has left me with a vehicle repair bill amounting to {amount of bill}. I would very much appreciate it if you would send me a check for that amount, as

it was clearly your car that struck mine. I am enclosing a photocopy of the bill, so that you can see a breakdown of the costs.

If you have any questions, please do not hesitate to call me at the phone number above. I truly appreciate your prompt attention to this matter, and I am sure we can work everything out in a calm and civil fashion.

Thank you very much.

Sincerely

Your Name

If you do not receive any kind of a response from the other person at this point, or if the other person simply refuses to pay you, then you will probably have to take him or her to court. In order to do so, you should look up the number of the local courthouse in the phone book, and explain your situation to the person you speak with. They will help you get the appropriate paperwork for small claims court, and they will also explain how you should deliver a summons to the other person. A summons is an official court document indicating that you are asking another person to meet you in a court of law in order to settle a dispute. The laws for delivering a summons vary drastically from state to state, so I cannot tell you the exact procedure here.

The court will assign you a date for a trial. You must attend that trial. If you do not show up at the time of the trial, and you do not have a valid excuse for being absent or late, then you will automatically lose. If anything comes up at the last minute that prevents you from attending, always call the court and explain your situation. They will try to reschedule your trial for you.

When you arrive in court, always dress nicely. Don't show up in jeans and a T-shirt. Wear a suit or a nice dress. Whenever the judge asks you a question, respond politely. Refer to the judge as "Your honor." Never lose your temper in front of the judge. For example, when talking about the person who won't pay your repair bill, don't call him or her a jerk. Rather, say something like, "I believe that Mr. Smith should pay my repair bill because he hit my car." Always speak as simply and straightforwardly as possible, without throwing in any technical legal jargon that you might have learned. And *always* be as specific as you can, without omitting any important facts.

You are allowed to bring evidence to court with you. Bring any letters that you have written to the other person (such as the sample letter that was given earlier). If you are in a dispute over something that was damaged, such as in the example of the fender bender incident, you should also bring photographs of the damage and a copy of the repair bill. You can also ask witnesses to come with you. A witness is someone who was present at the time of the incident. If someone was in the car with you when you got hit, for example, that person would also be allowed to give an account of the incident to the judge. If you have a witness to the incident, but that witness cannot make it to the trial, then ask that person to fill out and sign an affidavit. An affidavit is simply a written testimony of what the witness would have said in court. An affidavit must be signed under penalty of perjury, which means that the witness swears that testimony is a truthful account of the incident. Affidavits need to be signed in the presence of a notary public. A notary public is a licensed official with the legal right to administer the oath of perjury at the time the affidavit is signed.

Small claims court trials are usually very brief, running only fifteen to thirty minutes. After the trial is over, the judge will take a few minutes to make a decision, and then inform you of that decision. Hopefully the decision will be in your favor. If, however, it is not, you should be a good sport about it. You should shake the other person's hand and congratulate him or her, and you should ask the judge if there is any way that the decision can be appealed. If an appeal is allowed to be made, then the judge will explain how you should go about doing so.

Municipal Court

The next category is called Municipal Court. This category is also limited by a dollar value of the dispute, usually around $25,000. But a lawyer is allowed to represent you here.

As you can see, the stakes are quite a bit higher. As a result, the technicalities of attending Municipal Court are much more complex, and most people find it helpful to speak with a lawyer. If, however, you insist on representing yourself, simply call up the courthouse and inform them that you wish to file a claim in Municipal Court. They will give you all the paperwork you need, and they will explain to you how to deliver a summons.

Although the idea of presenting an argument to an impartial judge holds true for this category as well, the rules surrounding municipal court vary drastically from state to state, so I cannot really go into them here. You will simply have to ask the court a lot of questions, until you know exactly what paperwork needs to be filled out. But a lawyer will already be aware of these rules, which is why most people seek legal help.

Superior Court

The next category is called Superior Court. Generally, the amount of money disputed over in Superior Court is in the hundreds of thousands of dollars, or more! As a result, almost no one ever represents themselves. If you are ever involved in a conflict where such large sums of money are at stake, I absolutely suggest you contact a lawyer as soon as possible!

Federal Court

The next category is called Federal Court. Federal Court deals with even higher stakes, so again I suggest that you get in touch with a lawyer.

Criminal Court

The last category that we will discuss is Criminal Court, which was alluded to earlier in this chapter. As the name implies, Criminal Court deals with crimes. Examples of crimes include robbing grocery stores or murdering people. The stakes in Criminal Court are much more serious than even the largest sums of money disputed over in Civil

Court. You see, rather than awarding someone a sum of money, the function of Criminal Court is to determine whether or not someone committed a crime, and therefore whether or not they should go to jail. In states where there is a death penalty, the court sometimes even has to determine whether or not someone should be put to death!

Very few people ever decide to represent themselves in Criminal Court. I probably don't even have to tell you this, but if you are ever accused of a crime and find yourself in Criminal Court, then the police will allow you to make one phone call. That phone call should either be to a lawyer, or to a loved one who can contact a lawyer on your behalf!

2

Family Law

As you can probably tell from the name of this chapter, the first specific type of law that we are going to examine is family law. Family law refers to just about any kind of legal action that needs to take place in order to protect your family unit. By protecting the family unit, I am referring to the duties that you have in order to assure that everyone will be well taken care of in the event of death, divorce, or any other unpredictable event.

Let's start with the basics of getting married.

Marriage Licenses

Before you have a wedding ceremony, the government must officially recognize that a couple is going to be married. In order for you to notify the government of your impending marriage, you must apply for a marriage license. This license can be obtained from most state government offices, and it is quite straightforward to fill out. The application will indicate whether or not you need to perform any other actions, such as getting a blood test. The application will also give you the exact deadline by when the marriage ceremony must be performed in order for the license not to have expired.

Name Changes

While this tradition is no longer as common as it once was, many women change their last name to that of their husband after they get married. If you are a woman, you need to decide in advance of the wedding whether or not you want to take your husband's last name. You see, when you sign the marriage license, you will be asked what last name you will have in wedlock. Also, if you intend to change your last name, don't forget to have your driver's license, credit cards, bank accounts, passport, and all other such documentation updated. The most important agency to notify is the Social Security Administration, as the name reflected on your Social Security card must be changed.

Rights and Responsibilities of the Individuals in a Marriage

When a couple gets married, they are viewed as a single unit by the government. They have certain rights as that unit, such as the right to file a joint income tax return (which lessens the amount of tax that each owes). But each individual within the unit also still has certain rights and responsibilities that cannot be transferred onto the other.

For example, if a man who is in tremendous debt gets married, then that debt is not transferred onto his wife. As a result, if the couple buys a house, and the house is officially bought in the name of the wife, then the house cannot be taken away in order to pay for the man's debts! Thus the man has the responsibility to pay off his debt, and he cannot pass that responsibility onto his wife.

There are certain assets that each individual brings into a marriage that belong strictly to that individual, and not to the spouse. If each individual has a car, for example, and as a general rule each individual uses only his or her car, then the cars clearly belong to the individuals, not to the couple. This gets a little bit tricky (as you will discover in the next section), but there is one kind of item that always belongs to an individual, and not to the couple: an inheritance. If your rich and eccentric Uncle Irving dies and leaves you ten million dollars, then you own ten million dollars, not your spouse. Thus, each individual has the right to maintain some separate property.

Rights and Responsibilities of Couples

In the last section, there was a cryptic reference to the complications of maintaining individual possessions in a marriage, and I will now elaborate on this point. Legally, there is a term called marital property. This property refers to any items that belong to the married couple, rather than one individual in the couple. Let's reexamine the example of the two cars that was given earlier. Now, let's suppose that each individual does not only use his or her own car; let's suppose that they share their cars so frequently, that it becomes difficult to tell which one belongs to which person. In that case, the cars have become marital property. Let's also take another look at the example of the inheritance. It is possible to make an inheritance into marital property, and there are certain tax advantages to doing so (these advantages must be discussed with an accountant, as that subject is far too complex for this book). If the individual who inherited the ten million dollars keeps it in his or her own private account, then it remains the property of the individual. But if the money is deposited into a joint account, which is held by both members of the couple, then it becomes marital property. Thus, the other individual will now have equal access to it.

If a couple buys anything together, then it is considered marital property, even if it is paid for entirely by one individual. Thus, if a man buys a car that is intended for both his use and the use of his wife, then it is marital property.

The individuals in a couple have the duty and responsibility to take care of each other. Just as is indicated in common marriage vows, couples need to help each other out "in sickness and in health, for richer or poorer." Thus, if only one individual in the marriage works, then he or she should support the other individual financially. If both members of the couple work, then they should pool their resources in order to attain the best standard of living possible. Therefore, if you inherit ten million dollars, you do not have to pay off your spouse's debts, but you must support them.

Common-Law Marriages

There is a legal term known as common-law marriage. This term refers to couples that have been living together for many years, and clearly interact in the same manner as a legally married couple, but simply do not have a marriage license. In this case, the members of the common-law marriage have all of the same individual and joint responsibilities that have been outlined above.

Prenuptial Agreements

Let us now turn to the topic of prenuptial agreements. Prenuptial agreements are a kind of contract that have been becoming more common over the past few years, especially among the rich and famous. The prenuptial agreement clearly sets forth in writing which property belongs to the individuals in the marriage, and which items are marital property. Thus, if a couple ever gets divorced, it is easy to figure out who gets what.

There are many special clauses which can be included in a prenuptial agreement, such as how any assets are to be apportioned if one of the spouses dies. Like all other contracts, prenuptial agreements are very sophisticated legal documents, and neither party should sign one without first consulting a lawyer. Many people feel that such agreements remove all of the trust from a relationship, one of the essential ingredients of a good marriage, so they refuse to have one. If one spouse wants a prenuptial agreement, but the other does not, then it might be an indication that the two would not make a very compatible married couple!

Many people feel that prenuptial agreements reveal an ugly sign of the times: that litigiousness is on the rise. Litigiousness means the frequency with which people engage in law suits. It is a fact that the more litigious a society is, the closer it is to its own downfall. Shortly before the fall of the legendary Roman Empire, for example, the number of lawsuits heard in their courts of law increased at an alarming rate. Many scholars view litigiousness as a sign that trust is becoming scarce and that greed is becoming more common, and they claim that such tendencies undermine the fabric of society. Therefore, if you intend to engage in a prenuptial agreement, then you should discuss the topic frankly and openly with your spouse. If you cannot even reach an agreement on this issue, what will you be able to agree upon during the marriage?

Now let's take a look at divorce.

Divorce

If you feel that your marriage is no longer working, and you wish to obtain a divorce, then there is a very specific procedure which you must follow in order to do so. First, you must have grounds, or reason, for a divorce. There are two categories of reasons: no-fault and fault. The categories are fairly self-explanatory; if you get a divorce for no-fault reasons, then you are recognizing that neither you nor your spouse is responsible for the failure of the marriage, whereas if you get a divorce for fault reasons, then you are indicating that you believe it is your spouse's fault that the marriage failed. The most common no-fault grounds for a divorce is irreconcilable differences, which simply means that two people can no longer get along with each other. The most common fault grounds include adultery, addiction to drugs or alcohol, and abuse.

Next, you need to file a complaint with the court, outlining your grounds for requesting a divorce. The complaint is then served on your spouse, and he or she must respond to it in writing. By this time, both you and your spouse will probably have hired lawyers to deal with the paperwork, which is definitely a good idea.

Working with both you and your spouse, your lawyers will try to divide the assets up in a way in which everyone approves. Once this has been accomplished, the proposed settlement will be sent to a judge to review. He or she may approve it or ask that it be revised somewhat in order to treat each individual more fairly.

If you and your spouse cannot divide up the assets in a way in which you both agree, then you will have to go through the agony of a divorce trial. This can become very messy and uncomfortable emotionally, so it is always best to try to avoid it if possible.

Now that you understand how a divorce proceeding is legally conducted, let's move on to some of the specific items you need to keep in mind if you feel the need to get a divorce. First, there is the issue of property. Please refer to the earlier section in the chapter on marital property versus individual property, as you will need to understand those concepts in order to understand the rest of this section.

If you have to go to trial because a settlement cannot be reached between you and your spouse, then the court will ask you to identify your individual property. This property will be distributed to the individual owning it, unless there is a good reason not to do so. For example, if your spouse has a car, but you do not, and you have more of a need for a car than he or she does, then the court might decide to give you the car. Then the marital property will be divided, which is a bit more tricky. If you live in a state where the notion of community property is legally recognized, then all marital property will be divided equally between the two individuals. If you live in a state where the notion of equitable distribution is legally recognized, then the court will try to distribute the assets as fairly as possible between the two individuals. Your lawyer will be able to tell you which type of asset distribution system is legally recognized in your state.

Some of the responsibilities of marriage do not dissolve once the marriage has come to an end. For example, the individuals still have the responsibility to support each other. If only one member of the marriage was working during the marriage, then he or she has to pay alimony to the other member after getting a divorce. Alimony is money that is intended to help out the spouse until he or she is able to find a job. If that job provides a significantly lower standard of living than the spouse had become accustomed to during the marriage, then alimony will still have to be paid.

The responsibility of looking after your children also does not end. First, it must be decided who gets physical custody of the children. Physical Custody is the legal term indicating which of the two parents will actually live with the children. The other parent has visitation rights, which means that he or she will only get to see the children for a limited amount of time each week, usually on weekends. It is very difficult to decide which of the parents should get physical custody of the children, and the court usually has to rely on such criteria as which parent will be able to spend more time each day with the kids. Until recently, physical custody was usually granted to the mother, but fathers have protested this as unfair in many cases. Courts across the nation have recognized this protest, and now it is much more common for fathers to get physical custody, with the mothers receiving visitation rights.

It is also becoming much more common for both parents to have joint physical custody. This does not mean that the parents each live with the children for three-and-a-half days per week. The children still live with one parent, but the other gets to spend much more time with them than just weekends.

Now that you understand the concept of physical custody, you must also become acquainted with the idea of legal custody. Legal custody simply refers to a parent's right to have input on the way in which his or her child is raised. For example, just because a child is in the physical custody of one parent, that does not mean that the other parent cannot play a part in making decisions for that child, such as what school the child attends. Unless there are very good reasons for not doing so, such as one of the parents being a child abuser, joint legal custody is generally given to both parents, even if physical custody is given to just one.

Once the matter of custody has been decided on, the parents are still responsible for providing their kids with food, shelter, and medical attention. Thus, in addition to alimony, child support money is usually paid by one spouse to another after the divorce. Naturally, the child support is paid to the spouse who has physical custody of the children, as that spouse must feed and clothe the children each day. *If you are ordered by the court to pay alimony or child support to your ex-spouse after a divorce, and you fail to do so, then you are breaking the law!*

If your ex-spouse owes you child support, but he or she is not paying for it, then the law will do everything it can to protect you. This is such a complicated issue that a whole book could easily be devoted to it, so I cannot elaborate on it any further within this volume. However, free information on the subject can be obtained by writing to the Department of Health and Human Services in Washington, DC. Their address is as follows:

Office of Child Support Enforcement
Administration for Children and Families
370 L'Enfant Promenade, SW
Washington, DC 20477

Of course, your lawyer will also probably be able to help ensure that your ex-spouse makes child support payments.

The parent with physical custody of the children has certain responsibilities to his or her ex-spouse. For example, that parent cannot deny visitation rights to the other without good reason for doing so. Also, that parent cannot move far away without the court's approval of such a move, as it would make it very difficult for the other parent ever to see the children.

If the parent with physical custody over the children dies, then the physical custody usually goes to the surviving parent. If, however, that parent was initially denied physical or legal custody for grounds such as being an abusive parent, then the court will try to find a guardian for the children. A guardian is someone who takes on all of the responsibilities of a parent toward a child without actually being that child's parent. Oftentimes, the court will appoint the children's grandparents as their legal guardians.

The final area of family law that we will cover is actually termed probate law by the legal community. Probate law is the area of law dealing with wills, but I have chosen to include it in the section on family law, as the people to whom you will your possessions will most likely be your family members.

Probate

A will is a very important document. It is a formal written record that clearly expresses how you want your belongings (legally termed your estate) divided up by your heirs, or surviving relatives. A will must be written in strict compliance with state laws, and it must be signed in the presence of an appropriate number of witnesses. You should consult a lawyer for the details of wills in your state.

If you die without a valid will, then you have died *in testate*. This is very bad, as it can prevent your loved ones from receiving the appropriate amount of your estate. Technically, the state might have the right to seize all of your assets! Moreover, if you have children who are under the age of eighteen, and you are the only surviving parent, then the state has the right to assign them a legal guardian. Thus, if you have someone special in mind for guardianship of your children should you pass away unexpectedly, such as a beloved aunt or uncle, then they should be named in the will.

Before I relate to you all of the technical details of the probate process, I want to state at this point that items bequeathed (or willed) to heirs are subject to very heavy taxation. Thus, if you have been bequeathed something by one of your recently departed relatives, you might want to consult an accountant on the matter, so as to figure out the best way to pay taxes on it.

The first step in the probate process is, naturally, death. Assuming a valid will has been drafted by a lawyer and signed by the decedent (the person who has died) and the correct number of witnesses, the process can run rather smoothly. The will should name an individual as executor of the estate, or the person who makes sure that everything is given out to the correct heirs as intended by the decedent. With the assistance of a lawyer, the executor must present the will and various supporting documents (which vary from state to state) to a court of law. The executor then contacts each heir named in the will, indicating that they have been bequeathed certain items.

This is where the probate process can get tricky. Anyone can challenge the validity of a will in court. Challenges usually come from disgruntled heirs who did not receive as much as they expected. Challenges can come even when the will has been drafted in strict accordance to all state laws. You might have heard the old line "being of sound mind and body" that usually commences a will. The challenger will generally assert that the decedent was not of sound mind and body when he drafted the will; in other words, he was not thinking correctly, and the challenger deserves more of the estate than the will indicates. If a will is ever challenged, then be prepared for a lengthy court procedure that could take months, or even years to resolve. It is then the duty of the executor and the lawyer that he has obtained for the estate to defend against the challenge in court. Unfortunately, such legal battles can be very draining financially. As the estate's lawyer is generally paid with money from the estate, the resulting legal costs can whittle away the value of an estate to much less than its original value.

If no one challenges the will, or once a challenge has been resolved, then the court allows the executor to complete his duties as assigned in the will. In other words, the executor makes sure that everyone named in the will gets everything that is coming to them, that all of the decedents unpaid taxes and debts are accounted for, and that any other loose ends are tied up. Often, since being an executor is such a time consuming affair, the will indicates a sum to be paid to the executor. He receives this sum when everything else has been taken care of.

At this point I want to discuss the complexities of choosing an executor. First of all, you should never name someone as your executor without asking them first. They have the right to decline performing such a function, in which case the court can arbitrarily name someone else to act as executor. You should choose someone that you know and trust, and remind them that you are asking them to perform this favor because of your faith and confidence in them. The executor must pay careful attention to details, and it is often helpful (but certainly not necessary) if that person has legal experience. So don't pick your addle-brained Aunt Fanny to be your executor, even if she is your favorite relative!

If the person you have named executor in your will actually dies before you do, and you neglect to update your will, then the court has the right to arbitrarily choose a new one for you. So always make sure to keep in touch with your named executor!

As for your beneficiaries, or the heirs to whom you bequeath items, the law allows you to name just about anyone you want. But, there are certain restrictions. Your spouse, for example, has a right to a certain percentage of your estate, so you can't simply give everything to Aunt Fanny. Your children also have certain rights. Thus, when drafting your will, you should speak very frankly with your probate lawyer about how you should divide up your estate.

Very frequently, when bequeathing the various items of your estate, you will be left with a remainder of your estate, legally termed residue or residuary estate. Generally, this residue is bequeathed to residuary legatees, or beneficiaries who have special entitlements. The residuary legatees are most often the spouse or children of the decedent. Before the residue is paid however, the correct fee must be paid to the executor.

In a very loose nutshell, this is all you need to know about family law. Be aware that law is very complex, and this chapter has simply provided you with a cursory overview of this area. Now, we shall turn to your rights as a consumer.

3

Consumer Rights

Have you ever heard the Latin phrase *caveat emptor*? Translated into English, this ancient Latin phrase dating back to the days of the Roman Empire means, "Let the buyer beware!" In other words, the legal system employed by the Ancient Romans favored the seller or merchant. If a product for sale was broken or defective, then it was up to the buyer to notice it.

If you're like me, then you probably feel that this is not a very fair system. You are not alone in that thought. You see, the modern legal system that we have in America today defends the buyer, not the seller. No one can sell you a product or service in this country under false pretenses. For example, if an item claims to have a money-back guarantee if you are not completely satisfied with its performance, then the company producing that item must honor the guarantee. If it does not honor the guarantee, then the company is guilty of false advertising.

Consumer rights is that part of the law which deals with your rights whenever you purchase a product or service. If you are shelling out good money, then you should be compensated with a reliable product or service.

This chapter will outline some of the instances when you can exercise your rights as a consumer.

As you will discover in the examples below, many of the laws and regulations discussed differ from state to state. Accordingly, you should just use these rules as general guidelines. For the answers to any specific questions, you will either have to consult an attorney or do some research in a law library.

Products

Most states mandate that any item for sale in a store have a legible price tag on it. Furthermore, in most cases, if the store has accidentally put an incorrect price on an item, the store must sell it to you at that price. For example, if a department store sells a pair of shoes for $100, but accidentally puts $50 price tags on them, then they must sell you those shoes for $50.

Some states do allow stores to sell items without prices on them. You might have gone into a store where items were marked with a code, rather than with a price. As such, you had to ask the store manager how much each item cost. Although such stores are not necessarily dishonest, I personally do not enjoy patronizing such establishments, as I am not sure if I am being quoted an honest price.

Generally, unless you buy perishable items (such as food), most states allow you to return those items to the store where you bought them as long as they are still in their original condition. Usually, you must return the original receipt with the item, and some items must still be in their original shrink wrapping.

Stores are allowed to pay you back in whichever fashion they choose. In other words, they can either give you a refund or give you credit toward the purchase of another item at the store. If they give you a full refund, then the refund will generally take the form of the original payment. If you pay with a credit card, then they will usually credit the money back to your account. If you pay with cash, then they will give you cash back. If you pay by check, then they will cut you a check (this last method may take up to two weeks, as stores have the right to mail you the refund check).

Services

You will find that some other chapters in this volume refer to services that you can purchase. This is because of the complexities associated with each type of service. For example, your rights to service from a doctor differ from your rights to service from an attorney. The service that each of these types of professionals provides is discussed in other chapters.

In this chapter, I have decided to focus on services related to traveling. Millions of people go on vacation every year, and it is important to know your rights as a traveler.

Travel Agents

One of the biggest expenses that most people budget for each year is holiday traveling. Since taking your well-earned vacation each year can be so expensive, most people rely on the services of travel agents in order to get the best deals on airline tickets, cruises, hotel rooms, and resort accommodations. Most travel agents in this country are legitimate business people; they have spent years building up relationships within the travel industry, and they can legitimately help you find a great deal which you might not have been able to find on your own.

However, it is possible that you could come across a travel agent who does not truly have your best interests in mind. To help protect your rights, most states across the country have enacted laws outlining how a travel agent interacts with you. For example, in most states your travel agent must provide you with your airline ticket no more than two days after you have actually paid for the tickets.

Regrettably, most travel agents are not regulated by any agency or government body. Thus, most of the laws regarding travel agents simply dictate the timeliness with which they must provide you with your tickets once you have paid for them. If, for example, your travel agent promises to book you into a hotel with exquisite restaurants, and the only food you can actually get turns out to be sandwiches from room service, then your only definite recourse is not to use that travel agent any more. You might call the Better Business Bureau and ask that organization if they can lend you a hand. If the travel agent made so many misrepresentations that you did not get your money's worth for your vacation, then you might be able to take him or her to small claims court. Again, this is something you should discuss either with the Better Business Bureau or with an attorney.

Remember that your travel agent cannot be held accountable for things outside of his or her control. If you are planning to go on a romantic vacation to Hawaii, and rain and floods damage your hotel, then that is not really the travel agent's fault. However, the travel agent should be willing to help you get your money back from the hotel! Accordingly, if you ever have any trouble with your travel agent, the first step is to speak with him or her about it. Using the example of the previous paragraph, perhaps the travel agent legitimately thought that you were being directed toward a hotel with exquisite restaurants. He or she might be just as shocked as you are upon learning that such restaurants do not actually exist. In that case, the travel agent might be able to help you get some or all of your money back from the hotel.

Airlines

Perhaps you remember a time, about twenty or thirty years ago, when airline travel was a thing of luxury, when an airplane ride was an exciting adventure. If you've been on an airplane within the past few years, however, then you should be aware that airline travel is now just one big hassle. Planes are overcrowded and cramped, airports are fast-paced and unfriendly, and you're never sure if your baggage is going to arrive safely at your destination. So what are your rights amidst all this chaos?

The first thing you should be aware of is that you can't really hold an airline accountable for any delays. Delays are generally caused by weather (which is beyond the control of the airline), airport conditions (which are again beyond the control of the airline), or because of safety checks (which are more important than on-time arrivals). Therefore, if your plane is ever delayed, just sit back with a magazine and try to enjoy yourself as much as possible.

If a delayed flight results in your missing a connecting flight, then your airline must put you on the next available flight to that destination. I have never heard of an airline refusing to do so. However, you might have to wait for a few hours before such a flight is available.

You might have heard about people being bumped from their flights. Bumping happens when too many people are booked onto the same plane. Airlines allow this to happen because they know that there is a very high chance that at least 5% of the passengers will cancel their tickets at the last minute. If such cancellations do not occur, however, then someone will have to relinquish his or her seat. First, the airline will ask if anyone will relinquish his or her seat voluntarily. In exchange for this, the airline must offer you some sort of compensation, such as a free ticket to be used on a later journey. If not enough people volunteer to be bumped, then the airline has the right to bump passengers at random. In exchange for this, the airline must offer you the same compensation that was offered to the volunteers.

If you have ever bought an airline ticket yourself, then you've probably noticed a lot of fine print that accompanies any low price offer. Generally, an airline can attach as much fine print to a ticket as it wants. In other words, an airline can declare that a ticket is non-refundable, and that the time and date of the flight cannot be changed (or can only be changed with a nominal surcharge). Therefore, before you buy a ticket, you should do your best to make sure that it meets your exact requirements, because you might not be able to exchange it later.

If you ever have any serious complaints with the way you are treated by an airline, then there are several agencies which can help you. They are the Department of Transportation and the Federal Aviation Administration, and they can be reached at the following addresses:

United States Department of Transportation
Office of Consumer Assistance
400 Seventh Street, SW
Washington, DC 20590

Federal Aviation Administration
Office of Consumer Affairs
APA-200, 800 Independence Avenue, SW
Washington, DC 20591

Moving Companies

Moving all of your household items is generally a very expensive prospect, costing in the thousands and thousands of dollars. As such, the law understands how important a move is to you, and it serves to protect you in case a moving company ever loses or damages any of your items.

It is always in your best interest to speak with several moving companies before deciding upon which one to trust with your personal belongings. *Do not do business with any moving company that will not give you an estimate in writing.* Also, most states require moving companies to sign written contracts with their customers. Therefore, you should ask to see a copy of the standard contract in advance, to make sure that you understand any fine print or details about the move. Most states also require moving companies to provide their customers with booklets outlining their rights. The contract will state such details as the time and date when the movers have to pick up and deliver your property. Be sure to ask the moving company about the rights your state affords you if the moving company does not comply with these details.

There are two kinds of estimates that you can receive: binding and non-binding. A binding estimate is one which states that the final cost of the move cannot exceed the costs outlined in the estimate. However, you may be charged for this estimate, and the fee differs from company to company. A non-binding estimate is one which states that the cost of the move can exceed the costs outlined in the estimate, but the estimate itself is free. Generally, however, there is a ceiling as to how much the actual cost can exceed the non-binding estimate, so you should discuss this with the company.

Any legitimate moving company will make an inventory of your items as they pack them up. This inventory is for your own protection, so you should keep careful track of it. If any of your property is lost or damaged, then the value of that property will be reflected on the inventory. If an item is lost or damaged, but it is not listed on the inventory, then the moving company is not obligated to assume responsibility for that item. Whenever you move, the moving company will offer you various levels of insurance to protect your goods; the cost of this insurance should be included in the estimate. It is up to you to decide how much insurance you are willing to pay for, and a moving company is not liable for payments beyond the amount of insurance. For example, if you buy $10,000 worth of insurance, and the moving company breaks an item valued at $15,000, then they only have to pay you back $10,000. Private insurance companies also sell moving insurance, so you might want to see if you can get a better deal by buying your insurance from someone else (but first make sure that your moving company allows outside insurance).

There is a national association which can help you if you ever have a dispute with your moving company. Its name and address is as follows:

American Movers Conference
Dispute Settlement Program
1611 Duke Street
Alexandria, VA 22314.

If your needs are better served by a state or local agency, then the American Movers Conference will be able to refer you to that agency.

included in the estimate. It is up to you to
decide how much insurance you are willing
to pay for, and a moving company is not liable for payments beyond the amount of insurance. For example, if you buy $10,000
worth of insurance and have a shipment
valued at $15,000, then they
only have to pay you up to $10,000. Private
insurance companies also sell above-insur-
ance to protect them. Even if you can get
a better deal by buying your insurance from
someone else (but make sure that your
moving company allows outside insurance).

There is a national association which can
help you if you ever have a dispute with your
moving company. Its name and address is as
follows:

American Movers Conference
Dispute Settlement Program
1611 Duke Street
Alexandria, VA 22314

If your needs are better served by a state or
local agency, then the American Movers Conference will be instructed you to that agency

4

Owning and Operating Motor Vehicles

Owning and operating a motor vehicle is a very serious affair. Whenever you set out on the road, you are encasing yourself in a vehicle that could potential harm or kill many innocent bystanders. Utmost care is required when driving, and the law is very strict about your rights and responsibilities toward others on the road.

Driver's Licenses

The most basic law to which you must conform when driving is having a driver's license. The license is simply permission from the state in which you reside to operate a motor vehicle. The following are the basic requirements for attaining a driver's license:

1. You must be able to demonstrate your knowledge of the rules of the road by passing a written test.

2. You must be able to demonstrate your ability to operate a vehicle with care by passing a practical driving test under the supervision of a state-licensed tester.

3. You must be able to demonstrate a mini-

mum quality of eyesight by passing a vision test. You may pass this test conditionally; for example, you may be permitted to drive so long as you wear glasses.

4. You must be at least sixteen years old.

There are different types of licenses for the operation of different types of vehicles. Just because you are allowed to drive a car does not mean you can drive a motorcycle or a truck. When applying for a license with the department of motor vehicles, be sure to specify which type of license you want.

Licenses are specific to each state. Therefore, if you move from one state to another, be sure to change your driver's license. Usually, you will not be asked to pass another road test. You will simply have to pass the written test, indicating your mastery of the laws of the road for that state. You will then be asked to turn in your old driver's license, and you will be given a new one.

Licenses are not permanent. They are generally valid for a four year period. When you are nearing the expiration date of your license, you should contact the Department of Motor Vehicles (DMV) and inquire as to the procedure for obtaining a new one. Depending upon your driving record, you may be automatically issued a new one, or you may have to take the written test again. Your driving record is a list of any traffic violations, or tickets, you have received. Examples of violations include speeding, failing to stop at a red light, and driving while intoxicated. The latter is a very serious offense.

If you get too many moving violations, then your license could be suspended or revoked for a certain period of time. Depending upon the state you live in, you might still be allowed to drive to and from work during the suspension periods. If your license is ever suspended, then you will have to appear before a judge in a court of law, and all of your rights during the suspension period will be explained to you. We will discuss violations in more detail shortly.

Vehicle Registration

You must register your motor vehicle with the DMV of the state in which you live. In order to register your vehicle, you must call the DMV and ask for a registration form. You will receive detailed instructions for filling out the application, including explanations of any supporting material that must be sent along with the application.

There are several reasons why you must register your vehicle. First, registering your vehicle enables the DMV to have a record of it. That way, if it is ever stolen, the police will have instant access to all records about the car, including its license plate numbers. Second, registering your car is a way of paying your highway taxes. You see, when you register your car, you will be asked to send in a check, the amount of which varies from state to state. Part of this money is often applied to the state's highway fund, enabling state governments to keep highways in good repair.

When your registration has been processed by the DMV, you will be given a license plate. If you live in a state that mandates both front and rear license plates, then you will be given one for each location. You will also be given a sticker to place on the rear plate, indicating the date when the registration will expire. Just as with your driver's license, your vehicle registration has an expiration date. The DMV will send you a letter notifying you when you need to renew your registration. Thus, if you move to a new residence within the state where your car is registered, you should inform the DMV of your new address.

If you move to a new state altogether, then you will have to re-register your car in that state. You should do some research into the laws regarding moving a car from one state to another. California, for example, has very strict laws for carbon monoxide emissions, known as smog laws. Cars sold in other parts of the country generally do not meet the standard set by California. In order to discourage people from other states from bringing their cars with them when they move to California, that state's DMV imposes very high fines on cars that do not pass its smog laws. Thus, if you try to register a vehicle in California that was bought elsewhere, you could have to pay a very expensive fine. As a result, it might be cheaper for you to sell your car before moving to California, and then buy a new one upon arrival.

Moving Violations

Whenever you are stopped by a police officer while driving your car, you are being stopped for conducting a moving violation. There are very strict laws surrounding the operation of a motor vehicle on public roads, and you must conform to these laws. Failure to do so is considered a moving violation. A moving violation is technically a criminal offense, but most moving violations carry such small penalties (such as fines of $100 or so), that there is no social stygma attached to them.

If you have a driver's license, then you are probably already familiar with most of the laws of the road. For example, you may not exceed a posted speed limit. You may not pass through an intersection without stopping behind a stop sign. You must always wear your safety belt. You must stop at a red light.

When a police officer stops you, he will ask to see your driver's license and vehicle registration. In some states you will also be asked to show proof of vehicle insurance (more about this later). Police cars across the nation are now equipped with computers that are able to call up DMV records instantly. Using this computer, the officer will be able to make sure that you are not driving a stolen car, and he will also be able to see whether or not you have received any moving violations in the past. If you have not received one in the past, then he may use his discretion and simply give you a warning, without actually giving you a ticket.

If he does feel that you should be given the ticket, however, he will explain to you the law which you have broken. He will also ask you to sign the ticket, indicating that you have received it.

You have two options at this point. First, you can pay the ticket, admitting your guilt in the situation. The ticket itself will have instructions for making payment. Do not try to pay the officer in person, or he might mistake this as an attempt to bribe a police official, which is a very serious crime. If you admit your guilt, then there is a chance that your insurance premium will be raised (again, more on insurance later).

Your second option is to fight the ticket in traffic court. Traffic court is essentially run just like small claims court, but it only deals with moving violations. For a summary of the workings of small claims court, please refer to chapter one. That chapter will provide you with complete instructions for bringing evidence and witnesses to court. The two parties in any traffic court action are the plaintiff, or the police officer who gave you the ticket, and the defendant, or you. The ticket will have detailed instructions printed on it explaining how you can go about fighting the violation in court.

Why should you fight a ticket? Simply put, because you think you were ticketed unfairly. Police officers are human beings, just like you and me, and they are susceptible to making mistakes. For example, if you receive a ticket for running a red light, but you truly believe the light was still yellow when you passed through the intersection, then you have the right to fight the ticket in court. Just like with more serious criminal cases, you are considered innocent until the police officer can prove you to be guilty. Therefore, the judge in traffic court will have to base his ultimate decision on either your word, or the word of the police officer.

You should be aware that, as a general rule, traffic court judges are more likely to believe the word of police officers. You see, police officers are trained observers, and are thus more unlikely to make mistakes than you are. Therefore, if you want to make your testimony outweigh that of the police officer, you should try to get a witness to corroborate, or agree with, your side of the story. If someone was in the car with you when you received the ticket, then that person can act as your witness.

If you want to fight a ticket in court, you should always pay close attention to the violation that the police officer wrote down on the ticket. It is not uncommon for officers to write down the wrong violation by accident. If, for example, the police officer stopped you for running a stop sign, but he writes down that he stopped you for running a red light, then you can challenge the ticket on the basis that there is no traffic light at the intersection where you were stopped! Using this example, it would be a good idea for you to take a picture of the intersection and bring it to court with you as evidence. That way, you can illustrate to the judge that you are being accused of a crime that you did not commit!

Unfortunately, the way in which the type

of violation is indicated on the ticket is a bit complicated. Rather than writing down the words "Ran a red light," the officer will write down a series of numbers. These numbers are the reference numbers for traffic codes or laws. In order to determine whether or not the officer has written down a correct number for the violation that he has accused you of, you will have to make a trip to a local law library. Many universities have such libraries on their campuses. You can ask one of the librarians for help in searching for the number in the many volumes of state traffic codes.

If you decide to fight a ticket in court, and the officer forgets to show up in court on the appointed day, then you will win the case by default! When you win a case in traffic court, whether by default or by proving that you were ticketed incorrectly, the violation will be removed from your DMV record. Therefore, your insurance premium will not be raised.

Driving While Intoxicated

Driving while intoxicated is one of the most serious moving violations that you can commit. This offense is commonly referred to as drunk driving, and it results in the deaths of hundreds of innocent motorists each year! Simply stated, you should never drink and drive.

What does it mean to be driving while intoxicated? In legal terms, your blood alcohol level must be greater than .05 to .10 percent, depending on the state in which you live. For most people, this level translates to roughly one drink per hour. In other words, if you have one drink, then in general you should wait at least one hour before you drive. If you have two drinks, then you should wait at least two hours. A drink is either a can of beer, a glass of wine, or a shot of hard alcohol.

There are two ways in which a police officer can stop you for suspected drunk driving. First, if you are driving very poorly, such as weaving in and out of lanes, then the police officer has probable cause to stop you. Probable cause means that due to the observable evidence, there is a very high chance that you are driving while intoxicated. Second, if you are stopped for committing another violation, and the officer smells alcohol on your breath, then the officer can suspect you of drunk driving.

If you are stopped for suspected drunk driving, then you have certain rights. You will be asked to perform a test of coordination, such as walking a straight line or touching your nose with your finger, but you have the right to refuse to do so in most states. If you refuse to do so, however, this will be viewed by a court of law as probable guilt on your part. You will also be asked to engage in a scientific test to determine your blood alcohol level, but you have the right to refuse to do so. Usually, the test will take the form of a breathalyzer, which is a device that you blow into. The breathalyzer is an extremely well calibrated device, and it rarely reports an incorrect blood alcohol level. But if you refuse to take a breathalyzer test, in most states your license will be suspended, and a court of law will view your refusal as evidence that you probably were drunk. Therefore, at the very least you will lose your license, and at the most you will probably be convicted of drunk driving anyway.

But, there are certain procedures that you do not have the right to refuse. For example, if you are involved in an automobile accident, and the police have reason to believe that you are drunk, then they can administer a scientific test to you without your permission. In the case of an accident, especially when someone has been hurt or killed, they will probably take a sample of your blood, rather than giving you a breathalyzer test.

If you are arrested for drunk driving (in which case you will actually be arrested, and not simply receive a traffic ticket), then you will have to go to court. As drunk driving is such as serious offense, it should not be handled with the lightness of other traffic related charges. It is *always* best at least to consult with a lawyer prior to going to court, and it is probably best to have a lawyer represent you at your trial.

So what are the penalties for drunk driving?

They are probably more severe than you ever realized. If you are found guilty of drunk driving then you could receive any or all of the following punishments:

1. Suspension of your license for up to three years.
2. A fine of up to $5,000.
3. A prison sentence of up to 2 years!

Your automobile insurance will also undoubtedly become much more expensive (insurance will be covered in more detail in the next section). If you are found guilty of drunk driving a second time, then the penalties are even worse:

1. Suspension of your license for up to five years.
2. A fine of up to $10,000.
3. A prison sentence of up to 2 years.

If you are found guilty of drunk driving three or more times, then you could face the following:

1. Permanent suspension of your driver's license.
2. A fine of up to $150,000.
3. A prison sentence of up to six years.

Note that these punishments are for cases where no one has been hurt and no damage has been caused. If any harm or damage arises from your drunk driving, then the penalties are much more severe. If, for example, someone died as a result of your drunk driving, then you could be charged with manslaughter, which is essentially unintentional murder!

As an aside, you should be aware that the responsibility for refraining from driving while intoxicated rests squarely on the shoulders of the individual. In other words, if you get intoxicated at a bar, you cannot use the excuse in court that the bar should not have sold you so many drinks. While many states throughout the country now have laws which also hold the bar responsible for selling you the alcohol which caused you to drive drunk, those courts will *always* still punish you as well.

Insurance

Now let's move onto a slightly lighter subject than drunk driving: car insurance. (I bet you never heard of car insurance being referred to as a light subject before!).The law says that you must have car insurance, in case you cause an accident and damage needs to be paid for.

There are two kinds of car insurance. The

first is known as liability insurance, and it covers the costs of any damages to the other cars involved in an accident if you cause the accident. The damages that it covers may be either to the car itself, or to the passengers in the other car. Generally, the minimum amount of liability insurance that you are allowed to have is $35,000. Depending on where you live, the premium, or the amount of money that you have to pay to the insurance company to receive this coverage, can be very expensive or very cheap. If you live in a large metropolis, such as Los Angeles or New York City, where there are thousands of cars and hundreds of accidents occur each day, then your premium will be pretty expensive. If you live out on a farm in the middle of the country, on the other hand, then your premium will probably be quite low. Liability insurance is the kind of car insurance that is mandated by law.

If you have enough money to pay an expensive premium, then you can often buy liability insurance that can cover you for damages of over $1 million! While sums this huge will more than cover any hospital bill or car repair bill for which you will be held liable, it can help protect you in the event of a lawsuit. You see, if you hit another car, then the other driver could sue you on the basis of emotional scars or longterm suffering as a result of the accident. This is the kind of lawsuit that you often hear about on TV, which can literally ruin you financially. If someone sues you for $1 million, but your insurance will only cover you up to $35,000, then where are you going to get the extra money? Thus, just to be on the safe side, many drivers elect to get very expensive insurance policies.

While the law insists that you have this type of insurance, it does not insist that you purchase your insurance from one specific company. As a result, you have the right to shop around for the best rates. You should be aware that the younger you are, the more expensive your premium will be. Also, if you have received any traffic violations or have been involved in any previous accidents, then your policy will cost you more. Additionally, it is more expensive for a man to receive insurance than it is for a woman. The reason for these price discrepancies is that statistics prove that more men get into accidents than women, more young people get into accidents than older people, and people with numerous traffic violations tend to cause more accidents.

When buying your insurance policy, ask them if they have any discounts that might apply to you. For example, if you are a student with an outstanding academic record, then you might qualify for a reduced rate. If you were ever an Eagle Scout, then you could also get a discount. If you were in the military, then your premium could be lowered. Characteristics such as these prove to an insurance broker that you are a reliable and trustworthy person, not likely to cause an automobile accident. Therefore, it is unlikely that the insurance company will ever have to pay lots of money to another driver on your behalf.

You should be aware that there are very serious fines for driving without liability insurance. The fines differ from state to state, but they frequently run into the thousands of dollars. In most states, police officers now have the right to ask for proof of insurance if they ever stop your car for a routine traffic violation. If they discover that you do not have insurance at that time, then you will be held responsible for paying such a fine. In short, never drive without insurance; not only is it irresponsible and inconsiderate to other drivers, but it also always works out to be more expensive in the long run!

Whenever you buy liability insurance, you should also ask the insurance broker how much the deductible is. There is no such thing as a free ride, and even though they will pay for most of the damages, they will still probably make you pay for at least a certain amount. Common deductibles range from $500 to $2,000.

The second type of insurance is called comprehensive and collision. This is the insurance that covers you and your vehicle in the event that you cause an accident. This type of insurance is not mandated, as it is for your protection, rather than the protection of others. Typical coverage extended by comprehensive and collision insurance starts at around $15,000, and the premium is far less expensive than the liability premium. Comprehensive and collision insurance also covers you if your car gets stolen, or if it gets broken into.

There is a third type of insurance that exists in some states known as uninsured driver insurance. This type of policy will cover you in the event that your car is hit by a driver who does not have insurance. These policies are usually quite inexpensive, so you should discuss them with your insurance broker.

There is just one more thing you need to know about automobile insurance: the kinds of coverage you get varies from state to state. Some states have what is known as a no-fault system, while others use the fault system. In no-fault states, for minor accidents such as fender-benders, each driver recovers the cost of damages from his own insurance company. It does not matter who caused the accident. In states with the fault system, one driver is always assigned the responsibility of causing an accident, no matter how small, and his insurance company must pay for any damages. For serious accidents, or for any accident in which someone is hurt, then the fault system automatically comes into effect, even in no-fault states. Thus, if you get hurt because someone else rear ends you, then that person's insurance must pay for your hospital bills, even in a no-fault state.

Accidents

So now that you know about insurance, what exactly are your legal responsibilities if you ever get into an accident?

Your first responsibility is to make sure that everyone is unharmed. If someone looks like they have been hurt, then don't try moving that person. You see, if they have hurt their spinal cord, moving them could inadvertently cause paralysis. You should wait for an ambulance to arrive, because the medical technicians have special equipment that can move someone safely.

Once everyone's safety has been ascertained, you need to assess the damage to the vehicles. If possible, you should try not to move the cars, as this could destroy evidence indicating who was at fault in the accident. In this case, you should try to place flares around the accident site, so that other motorists will be warned to keep clear of a potentially hazardous area. And you should also stay out of the road, as it is not uncommon for someone who is standing in the road to get struck down by a passing car! This is especially true at the scene of an accident, when other drivers are curious about the damage they are seeing, and are not really paying attention to the road.

If the damage to the vehicles looks like it totals less than $500, then you should exchange names, phone numbers, addresses, driver's license numbers, insurance company names, insurance company phone numbers, and insurance policy numbers with the other driver. Never let someone leave the scene of an accident without providing you with this information! Your insurance company will need all of this information in order to process any claims. As long as you have this information, you can move the cars and continue on your way.

But if anyone has been hurt as a result of the accident, then you must call the police. The police will come and make a detailed report of the accident, so that this information can be furnished to the insurance companies. You are breaking the law if you fail to call the police!

5

Your Home

There are two main ways in which you can pay to occupy your home. The first way is renting. Renting is when you pay the owner of a residence for the privilege of occupying that residence. Generally, you pay your rent every month, and there is often a minimum number of months during which you must occupy the residence. The second way is owning. Owning is when you actually purchase the residence, making it yours for life. Each of these two methods has many legal ramifications, so this chapter will be divided into two main sections, each of which covers one of the methods. Will begin with owning a home.

Brokers

Buying a home is just like buying any other object. You see one that you like, you pay a certain amount of money for it, and it becomes your property. Naturally, houses are much more expensive than most other items, which does tend to complicate the process a bit, but as long as you keep this basic concept in mind, you should not get confused by anything you read in this section.

Since the process of selling a home is such an emotional and difficult experience, most sellers rely on the service of brokers. Brokers are real estate agents who actually spend time showing the house to potential buyers; brokers try to make the deal happen. Brokers earn their living by taking a percentage of the money that the seller receives after the house is sold. This percentage is usually somewhere around 6%. Thus, if your broker sells your home for you for $100,000, then he or she has earned a commission of $6,000.

When you hire a broker, you will probably sign an agreement with him or her. An agreement is a simplified contract. Make sure that the agreement is phrased in such a way that the broker only earns the commission after the completion of the sale. That way, if the potential buyer backs out at the last minute after making an offer, you won't owe your broker any money! Another thing to remember is that the broker only earns a percentage of the actual sale price. Therefore, if you offer your home for sale at $100,000, but have to end up reducing the price to $90,000 in order to sell it, the broker earns 6% of $90,000, and not 6% of $100,000.

Of course, you do not need a broker. You can try to sell a home by yourself — you've probably seen one of those signs that reads "For Sale By Owner." You will be able to ask for less money, since you won't have to pay a broker's fee, which means your home will be more attractive to potential buyers. However, you probably won't be able to dedicate as much time to selling your home as a broker can, which means that the whole process could take considerably longer.

Buyer and Seller

Whenever you buy something, what is it that you want? You want a product that will not malfunction or break, that is a good value, and that does not have any strings attached. Whenever you sell something, you want to receive the best offer possible, and you want to make sure that the buyer pays the amount that he has promised to you.

There are two types of documents that you should be aware of before you embark upon buying or selling a home. The first is called a deed. A deed is the legal definition of a certain piece of property. For example, a deed will specify the exact boundaries of a piece of land, and it will indicate if any other person has ownership rights of any kind to the piece of land or anything on it. For example, it is possible for you to buy a piece of land without buying the house on it. The deed in the sale of a house should specify that the house itself is part of the piece of property and is not owned by anyone else. The second document is called the title. The title indicates the name of the owner of the piece of property. When you buy a house, the old owner will transfer these documents to you.

As the sums of money involved in the sale of a house are so great, a written contract is always involved. *No sale of real property (i.e., real estate such as houses) is legal or official in the United States without a written contract!!!!!!!* The contract should include the following information:

1. The name of the buyer and seller.
2. The exact piece of property being sold (as defined by the deed).
3. The amount of money for which the property is being sold.

4. The closing date (the date by which the old owner must vacate and hand over the deed and the title to the new owner).

Attorneys

At this point it is worth spending a few moments talking about the role of a lawyer during a real estate transaction. As you can see, the roles of the buyer and the seller are quite straightforward. As such, the kinds of agreements used when selling a house are typically also easy to read. However, there is a certain amount of caution that should be exercised. For example, clauses should be written into the contract regarding who is responsible for paying for any damage that occurs when the previous owner moves out. Therefore, while a lawyer is not absolutely necessary, I certainly suggest that you employ one to aid you in the purchase of your house. The specific type of lawyer you will need is called a real estate attorney. After all, your house is probably the single largest expenditure you will ever make.

Caveat Emptor

As I stated earlier, this old Latin saying means, "Let the buyer beware!" During the time of the ancient Roman Empire, the law was written in such a way that the buyer was always responsible for discovering any defects in the products he bought; when asked if a product was defective, the seller could even lie and indicate that there were no defects.

Buying a house in the United States does not work under exactly the same conditions, but you still need to "beware." You see, the seller is prohibited by law from making any misrepresentations regarding the house. Suppose, for example, that the seller is aware that the house has major structural damage due to an uncontrollable termite problem. If you ask him about the structural integrity of the house, and he says that it is fine, then he has knowingly misrepresented the facts to you, and has thereby nullified the agreement for you to buy his house. However, if he is not aware of the problem, and he truly believes the structure of the house to be solid, then the contract is valid, even if you eventually discover major termite damage. It is very difficult to prove in court that a seller has knowingly misrepresented the facts; the seller can always simply indicate that he was unaware of the problem.

Therefore, you should definitely have your house inspected by a professional assessor. Your real estate broker should be able to put you in touch with one. The assessor is a trained professional who will examine a house from head to toe, searching for any problems or defects. When his search is completed, he will give you a list of the problems, along with estimated costs for repairing them. At that point, you will have to negotiate with the seller about making repairs or about reducing the price of the home commensurately with the cost of hiring someone to repair it. If the seller refuses to make the necessary repairs or reduce the price of the house by a satisfactory amount, then the buyer can break the contract.

Now, I have to give you a warning about assessors. These people are not licensed by the government in any way. Therefore, if they make a mistake and overlook a major problem, you have no legal recourse against them. The most that you could possibly sue them for is the amount of their fee, not the cost of the repairs that they overlooked. Therefore, whenever hiring an assessor, you should ask for a list of references.

Contracts

In the previous section you learned one valid reason why a buyer can break a contract with a seller. A contract is a very serious agreement, and you cannot simply walk away from one on a whim. Therefore, you should not sign one unless you are absolutely positive that you want to buy the house. Typically, other than the reason indicated above, the only reason a buyer can break a contract is because he cannot obtain a mortgage from a bank (more on this later). However, the buyer will still be responsible for paying any applicable lawyers' and brokers' fees. If a buyer walks away from a contract without a valid reason, then the seller could sue the buyer for a considerable amount of money!

A seller generally cannot back out of a contract for any reason, even if he can't afford to buy a new home (he should have thought about this in the first place)! Once the contract has been signed, the seller cannot decide not to sell the house. In other words, by law the seller must move, or the buyer can sue him. If the seller has not moved out by the closing date (the prearranged date when all of the final steps of the transaction are completed and the buyer moves in), then the buyer can make the seller pay a substantial penalty. Your lawyer should be able to ascertain whether or not the contract is drafted correctly, containing all the appropriate clauses pertaining to a seller's failure to vacate promptly.

Mortgages

While the second volume of this set will have an entire chapter devoted to loans, credits, and other financial matters, no chapter on real estate would be complete without a cursory explanation of mortgages.

As most people do not have enough money to buy a house outright, they must get a loan from a bank. A mortgage is a type of loan that a bank makes to an individual in order to buy a house. Once you take out such a loan, you are responsible for paying back a certain amount of it each month, until you have paid back the entire amount. The amount of the loan itself is called the principal. Suppose you buy a house valued at $125,000. Using your life savings, you are able to make a down payment of $25,000 on the house. Therefore, you need a mortgage of $100,000. Based on your credit history (which will be discussed in greater detail in the next volume), a bank may decide to grant you this mortgage.

The reason that banks grant mortgage loans is that they end up making money by doing so. You see, in return for granting you the mortgage, they will charge you interest on the loan. Interest is an additional fee that you must pay to the bank whenever you make payments on the principal. Interest rates vary according to a variety of complex economic factors, but they are always based on a percentage of the principal that remains to be paid.

Mortgages always run for a specific period of time, usually twenty to thirty years. This means that you will have to make mortgage payments every month that you own the house, until the mortgage is paid in full. If you decide to move out before the mortgage is fully paid, then part of the money that you make when selling the house will go into paying off the remainder of the mortgage.

If you suddenly find yourself with some extra money, then you are allowed to pay off a larger chunk of your mortgage each month than you had previously agreed to. The incentive for doing this is that it will ultimately save you money; as the interest is based on a percentage of the principal remaining to be paid, then the more quickly you can pay off that principal, the less interest you will have to pay. If that sounds a bit complicated to you, then do not fret. Many people have difficulty when it comes to figuring out mortgage payments. If you have any questions about your mortgage, then simply call up the mortgage officer at your bank, and ask him to answer your questions.

We have just discussed what happens if you can pay more than your minimum payment each month. But what happens if you do not have enough money to pay the minimum amount on your mortgage? Can you promise the bank that you will make it up to them later? No! As I have already explained, banks make their money by the interest they charge on loans. Therefore, if you do not make your monthly mortgage payment (including the interest), then the bank loses money. And banks get very angry when they lose money. So what will happen to you if you don't make a payment?

To answer that, I must first define the term "collateral" for you. Whenever you ask a financial institution for a loan, you must give them something in return in order to make sure that you will not stop making payments on the loan. The item that you give them in return is called the collateral. When the type of loan is a mortgage, the house itself is the collateral. If you do not make a mortgage payment, then you are considered "in default" of the mortgage (which means that you have broken your side of the agreement). If this happens, then the bank has the right to seize your collateral. Therefore, the bank has the right to kick you out of your house and sell it to someone else! When a bank does this, it is called "foreclosing on a mortgage."

Generally, if you think you will be unable to make a mortgage payment, then the best thing to do would be to call up the bank and ask them how they want to proceed. Chances are, they will try to work things out with you.

Taxes

You may or may not be aware that all real property in the Unites States (such as houses and condominiums) are subject to local property taxes. These property taxes are used to keep the local infrastructure running; for example, property taxes are often used to pay for public schools and for the salaries of local officials.

Property tax is based on the value of your home. Someone whose house is worth $100,000 would pay less property tax than someone whose house is worth $200,000. The government will send an assessor to your house on occasion in order to generate an updated appraisal of the value of your house. Your house's value changes for several reasons:

1. Damage to your house causes the value to go down.

2. Improvements to your house causes the value to go up.

3. Natural market pressures make the value of a house rise and fall (for example, during rough economic times, people generally can't afford to buy new houses, so the values of all houses fall uniformly).

You should ask your accountant whether or not your property tax is deductible from your income tax. Depending upon the state in which you live, you may be allowed to take this deduction.

Renting

Rather than buying a place in which to live, you could opt to rent a house or apartment. The basic advantage to renting is that you do not have any of the responsibilities accompanying owning a property. For example, you do not have to pay for property tax, you do not have to sell the property in the event that you move, etc. The basic disadvantage to renting is that you do not have any of the rights that accompany owning a property. For example, you cannot paint the walls any color that you wish without first obtaining the permission of the landlord, or property owner. Also, many people feel that paying rent to a landlord is like throwing money away; they reason that you could be putting that money into a mortgage, which means that you will own the property when the mortgage is paid in full.

Let's discuss the basic procedures that go along with renting an apartment or house. First, let's deal with the lease:

The Lease

So you've been scouring the classified ads for an apartment for weeks now, and you've finally found one that you like. The landlord takes an instant liking to you, and he asks if you want to sign a lease immediately. You agree.

A lease is a written agreement between the owner and the tenant, or the person who will actually be residing in the apartment or house. A lease should always be in *writing*. According to the laws of some states, a lease is not valid if it is made orally. A lease should include the following information:

1. The name of the landlord and the tenant.

2. The price of rent, and the date when each rental installment is due (rent is usually paid monthly, with the check being due on the first of each month).

3. The amount of the security deposit (we will go into security deposits in more detail shortly).

4. If the tenant is allowed to bring in a pet, musical instrument, or water-filled furniture.

5. If the price of the rent will increase during the course of the lease.

6. Which utility bills the landlord is responsible for paying, and which the tenant is responsible for paying.

7. The duration of your tenancy (generally month-to-month, six month, or year-long).

8. The exact address of the premises.

9. If the apartment come furnished or unfurnished.

10. How many (if any) parking spaces are included.

11. If there is any charge for late payments of rent.

More often than not, a lease is a standardized agreement that is printed up according to applicable laws in the state in which you live. As such, a landlord may be willing to make slight modifications to the lease at your request. For example, a lease may be pre-printed for a year-long tenancy, but the landlord may be willing to reduce that period to six months. In order to make a change on a lease, you must simply cross out any information that is no longer valid, write in any new information (in layman's terms — you should not attempt to rewrite a lease as if you were a lawyer), and then initial the change. The landlord should also initial the change.

Security Deposits

Usually, whenever you rent a property, the landlord will ask you to pay a security deposit along with your first month's rent. This security deposit is intended to protect the landlord if you leave the place filthy and damaged when you move out. A security deposit is generally equal to one or two month's rent.

When you move out, the landlord has a fixed amount of time to assess any damages. This amount of time varies depending on the state in which you reside, but it is always less than a month. Once the landlord has made the assessment, he will subtract this from the amount of the security deposit that you paid to him, and then return the remainder to you. As such, you should always apprise your landlord of your new address when you move, so that he can send you a check. Accompanying the check, you should receive an itemized invoice, indicating any damage that had to be paid for. If you believe that he has made an error in assessing the deductions, then you should contact him. Try to work things out in a courteous and sociable manner. If, however, your landlord happens to be one of those stereotypical crooked landlords, then you could wind up having to take him to court. The jurisdiction for landlord-tenant disputes is almost always small claims courts, as the amounts in question rarely exceed $5,000. For instructions on taking someone to small claims court, please refer to chapter 1 of this volume.

One good way to prevent any misunderstanding regarding your security deposit is to set down in writing the conditions of the deposit in an addendum to the lease. For example, it is not uncommon for landlords to charge approximately $100 for general cleaning to every tenant when a lease is over. Does your landlord have this policy? If so, would he be willing to let you do the cleaning yourself, so that you can save the $100?

Another good way to prevent misunderstandings is to perform a "walk-through" with the landlord when you move out. By doing this, you will accompany the landlord when he makes his inspection to assess damages, and you will know exactly what he intends to charge you for. You can also voice any protests that you have at that time.

There are a few things that landlords are not allowed to charge you for when they return your security deposit. If you actually cause any damage, or if you leave the place so messy that he has no option but to hire a professional cleaning service, then he can deduct these amounts. But he cannot deduct the cost of normal wear-and-tear. For example, a carpet will never look as good as it did when you first moved in, because you have been stepping on it everyday of your tenancy. The landlord can take out enough money to steam clean the carpet, but he cannot charge you for the cost of replacing the carpet! Moreover, most states forbid a landlord from deducting cleaning fees from a tenant's security deposit if that tenant has lived in the same apartment for three or more years. For example, let's suppose that you move into an apartment and pay a security deposit of $500. Four years later, you decide to move out. You have caused a slight amount of damage, however, in the form of a broken window. The landlord assesses this damage to cost $50. Therefore, he must return to you $450, which means that he has deducted $50 for repairs to damage, but nothing at all for cleaning.

Finally, the landlord cannot charge you for any damage that was already present in the apartment when you moved in. You should take the time to inspect thoroughly any apartment that you are thinking of moving into. Look at the walls and ceilings to make sure there are no patches. Look at the floors, to make sure there are no tears in the carpet or gashes in the wood. You should document any damage in an addendum to the lease, in order to make sure that you will not be charged for this damage when you move out. But while we are on this subject, you should be wary about renting an apartment with serious damage. Even if you are not responsible for paying for this damage, it could be an indication that living in the apartment will not be a pleasurable experience. For example, if you detect patches on the ceiling, then the roof might leak when it rains.

Ending a Lease

If you decide to end a lease before it expires, then you are "breaking the lease." If you have no good reason for doing so, then you are still responsible for all of the rent that is due until the lease would normally expire. So, if you have a year-long lease with a landlord for a property that is rented out at the rate of $500 per month, and you decide to move out after just 6 months, then you owe the landlord $3,000 ($500 X 6 remaining months = $3,000). Whenever a tenant breaks a lease without justification, the landlord generally simply keeps all of the security deposit as his only compensation. Technically, however, he does have the right to take the tenant to court. The tenant would almost surely lose this court dispute, in which case he would not only be liable for the unpaid rent, but also for any court costs.

A tenant can break a lease without being punished so long as there is a valid reason for doing so. Valid reasons include the following:

1. The landlord does not perform any necessary repairs (more on this later).
2. The premises are not habitable (more on this later).

In this case, the tenant must notify the landlord in writing of his intention to vacate the premises, along with the specific reasons for vacating. The tenant must generally give the landlord at least one month's notice prior to moving out, so that the landlord has the opportunity to rectify the situation. If the landlord does not rectify the situation, then the tenant can leave the premises without any repercussions. Moreover, the landlord must refund all of the tenant's security deposit, except for any amount that is necessary to pay for damages or cleaning. If the landlord fails to return the tenant's security deposit, then the tenant can take him to court.

If a landlord decides to break a lease, then this is called eviction. A landlord can only evict a tenant for justifiable reasons. Justifiable reasons include:

1. If the tenant does not pay rent.
2. If the tenant is continually noisy or makes it unpleasant for other tenants to live in the same building.
3. Changing the locks on the doors without notifying the landlord.
4. Painting the apartment without notifying the landlord.
5. Bringing in pets without prior authorization.
6. Subletting an apartment without prior authorization (more on this later).

Before a landlord can formally evict a tenant, he must notify the tenant in writing that he is a candidate for eviction. The tenant must be given the opportunity to "shape up"; for example, if the tenant has not paid his rent, then he can do so at this time in order to avoid being evicted. If the tenant does not shape up, then the landlord has the right to go to court to obtain a warrant for eviction. This means that a court hearing will occur to decide whether or not the tenant should be evicted. The landlord must furnish the tenant with the time and date of the court hearing, as the tenant has the right to appear at that hearing and defend his actions. A judge will listen to both sides of the story, and then make a decision based on the information that has been presented to him. If either the tenant or the landlord neglects to show up at the hearing, then the judge automatically rules in favor of the party that is present. Thus, if the judge rules in favor of the landlord, then the tenant is officially evicted.

Living Conditions

In order for a landlord to rent out a property to a tenant, that property must be habitable. This means that the apartment or house must provide a premises which offers some minimum amount of shelter, privacy, and safety. Examples of problems with a residence that make it unhabitable include:

1. Leaky ceiling.
2. Broken windows.

3. Appliances or plumbing that do not work.
4. Holes in the wall.
5. Unsafe electrical wiring.

As you can see, the list above normally describes buildings that are on the verge of being condemned! Chances are, you will never run into a building quite this bad. But if an apartment starts to deteriorate to this point while you are the tenant, then your landlord has the obligation to fix any problems within a reasonable amount of time, or to allow you to break the lease with no negative repercussions to you. For example, if there is more rainfall than usual during the time in which you are renting out an apartment, and this rain causes holes to appear in your ceiling, then your apartment has become unhabitable. You should speak to your landlord immediately.

If your landlord is the kind of person who shirks his responsibility towards his tenants, then you could find yourself in a tricky situation. Chances are, he won't make the repairs. However, if you break the lease, chances are he will not honor his legal obligation to return your security deposit. So what can you do in such a situation?

Some legal experts suggest withholding rent until the problem is solved. This is not a widely accepted idea, however. You see, if the issue ever winds up going to court, your refusal to pay rent could be viewed by the judge as an act of bad faith; in other words, the judge could interpret your actions as a sign that you did not try to work things out peacefully.

The most common outcome of an apartment becoming unhabitable is that the tenant breaks the lease. As you can probably predict, the landlord generally does not return the security deposit. As such, the tenant must sue the landlord in small claims court. While this procedure can be time-consuming, the tenant can generally win back most of his or her security deposit in court. If this ever happens to you, just remember to maintain a file of evidence to take with you to court. Keep copies of any letters that you have delivered to the landlord regarding the problem, make a journal indicating times and dates that you have spoken with your landlord about the problem either over the phone or in person, and take pictures of the damage that is making the apartment unhabitable. Landlords do not like to go to court, as they frequently lose court battles, so the very threat of taking them to court sometimes makes them shape up their act. If you demonstrate to your landlord that you are aware of your rights, then he will likely make sure that he does not violate any of them.

There are certain repairs that a landlord *must* make. For example, in an apartment building, areas such as lobbies and hallways must be maintained by the management. Within each individual apartment, landlords are usually responsible for the following repairs and maintenance:

1. Painting.
2. Keeping the appliances in working condition.
3. Maintaining climate control devices, such as heating and air conditioning.
4. Exterminating any pests.
5. Making sure that the plumbing works.
6. Making sure that the ceiling is sound.
7. Making sure that all electrical outlets are safe.

If you experience any of the above problems, then you should make a written request for a repair. Some landlords ask their tenants to fill out special "repair slips," while others simply make do with a letter that spells out the details. The landlord then has a "reasonable period of time" in which to make the repairs, generally one month or so.

There are a few exceptions to the landlord's responsibility, however. If the repairs are necessary due to the actions of the tenant, then the landlord does not have to pay for the repairs. For example, if your garbage disposal just stops working one day for no apparent reason, then the landlord should fix it. If, on the other hand, it stops working because you are shoving rice and pasta down it (*never* put starchy products down a garbage disposal), then you will be responsible for making the repairs.

Usually, landlords have relationships with one or two repair companies that they trust. As such, when you make a request for a repair, they will usually send "their repair guy over as soon as possible." However, some landlords do not have relationships with repair companies; in that case, when you make a repair request, they may authorize you to hire a repair man on your own, and then deduct the cost from your next rent. If they make such an authorization, then you should *ask for it in writing*. That way, they cannot conveniently "forget" that they allowed you to do so. Then, when you pay your next rent, you should also include a photocopy of the authorization and the original invoice outlining the costs of the repairs (keep a copy of this invoice for your records). The landlord will need this invoice in order to claim an income tax deduction.

If your landlord authorizes you to find your own repair man, then you should shop around for the best prices. You see, if the landlord feels that the bill you include with your rent is too costly, then he may refuse to allow you to deduct the amount from your rent. Technically, because you have a written authorization from him, he should not be allowed to do so, but you should do everything in your power to avoid conflicts.

If your landlord refuses to hire a repair man, and he refuses to authorize you to do so, then you are in a bit of a bind. As we discussed earlier, you could stop paying your rent, but this carries with it the risk of appearing that you have acted in bad faith. If the problem is severe, then you will probably have to break your lease, and then go through the hassle of getting your security deposit back.

Subletting

If you have a year-long lease, and you discover that you need to move out of town after just six months, then what can you do? Some landlords will allow you to sublet your apartment. This means that you allow someone else to occupy the apartment instead of you.

There are some problems associated with subletting an apartment. First, the landlord must be notified of your intent to sublet, and in most states he must authorize the action. Moreover, he has as much choice in the individual who takes your place as you do. In other words, if your best friend Skip wants to move in, the landlord can prevent him from doing so.

Additionally, sublets are generally handled in such a way that your name stays on the lease. As such, you are responsible for paying rent to the landlord. Then, you have to make sure that the sublettor pays you back.

If he does not do so, then you have the right to kick him out, but you are still left without the money that you need. Additionally, as you are on the lease, any damages will be billed to you, and you will have to be reimbursed by the sublettor. Therefore, you should never sublet an apartment to someone that you do not know and trust.

Discrimination

Landlords have a great deal of flexibility when deciding to whom they want to rent their property. However, their decisions must be made based on a reason that will affect a tenant's ability to live peacefully in a dwelling. For example, a landlord can deny an apartment to someone who earns very little money, as that person might not be able to pay the rent. Also, he can deny the dwelling to the members of a rock and roll band, as they could conceivably be playing their electric instruments all night long.

So when can a landlord not refuse to rent a dwelling to an individual? A landlord cannot refuse to rent out an apartment to an individual when that refusal is not based on a valid reason, such as the above. If a landlord refuses to rent out an apartment to someone for no valid reason, then he is guilty of discrimination. A landlord cannot base his decision not to rent a premises to an individual on any of the following reasons, or he will be in violation of laws protecting people from discrimination:

1. A tenant's religious beliefs.
2. A tenant's ethnic, national, or cultural background.
3. A tenant's gender.
4. A tenant's race.
5. A tenant's profession.
6. A tenant's marital status.

Notes

Notes

Notes